THE RAPTURE OF THE CHURCH

THE RAPTURE OF THE CHURCH

DENOTRA JOHNSON

PALMETTO
PUBLISHING
Charleston, SC
www.PalmettoPublishing.com

© 2024 Denotra Johnson
All rights reserved.
No portion of this book may be reproduced,
stored in a retrieval system, or transmitted in
any form by any means–electronic, mechanical,
photocopy, recording, or other–except for
brief quotations in printed reviews,
without prior permission of the author.

Paperback ISBN: 9798822949928

Table of Contents

The Tribulation: Are You Prepared? 1
Jesus Promised to Come Again 4
The Pre-tribulation Rapture 5
Bible Proof of the Pre-tribulation Rapture 6
Signs of the Timing of the Rapture 13
Events That Will Take Place before the Rapture of the Church 16
The Regathering of Israel 18
Knowledge Is Increased 19
Signs in Man 20
Signs in the Church 24
The Judgement Seat of Christ 25
Effects of the Rapture upon Christians Who Are in Heaven 32
The Choice Is Ours, Go or Stay! 35
Cause of the Tribulation 37
Man's Rebellion 37
The Day of the Lord 40
The Final Seven-Year Period of Daniel's "Seventy Weeks" 40
The Beginning of the Tribulation 41
The Rise of the Antichrist 42
The Rise of the False Prophet 43

The Sealing of 144,000 Jews 44
The Two Witnesses.. 44
The Wrath of God Poured Out 45
The Seven Seals Judgement 46
The Seven Trumpet Judgements 49
The Seven Vial Judgements 52
King Jesus Returns to Earth 56
Israel's Conversion 59
Christ Will Judge the Surviving Living................... 59
Christ Will Resurrect the Dead 60
Satan Is Loosed after a Thousand Years................... 60
The Great White Throne Judgement 61
The New Heaven and New Earth 64
Rapture, Ready or Not!.. 65
Jesus Is Coming, Are You Ready? 67
Scriptures Relating to the Rapture of the Church ... 70
About Rev. Denotra Johnson 73

The Tribulation: Are You Prepared?

The word "Rapture" is a word used by Christians to define the event described in the Word of God as the catching away by the Lord of His Church to be with Jesus Christ at the end of this church age. This is speaking of Christians being taken from the earth before the tribulation, which will begin immediately after the rapture, as all of God's blessings and protection will no longer exist on earth. This is one of the most significant and monumental events that will take place in the history of our world, and without question is the next most important event to occur on this planet. Why? Because this is when Jesus Christ will literally come down from heaven to get His beloved bride and take her to be with Him forever. In the Bible, God repeatedly instructs the Christians to be looking forward to that time when they will be taken into heaven and our salvation will be complete. We will finally be perfect, body, soul, and spirit, fit to fully and forever love and serve our Lord and one another in heaven and on earth.

1 Peter 1:13 *Fix your hope completely on the grace to be given to you at the revelation of Jesus Christ.*

Just think, *w*e will finally see the one who died for us while we were sinners and an enemy of His, so that we could be His Holy bride. And after loving and serving Him on earth, we could go to heaven and be with Him forever.

Col 3:4:11 *When Christ, who is your life, is revealed, then you also will be revealed with Him in glory.*

The event of the rapture is more relevant than ever before as we see all the end time events prophesied in the bible taking place. But because the word "Rapture" is not actually found in our present-day English translations of the bible, there are many Christians as well as non-believers who do not believe that the rapture is a biblical event that is going to take place. The word "Rapture" is more relevant than ever before, but where is it in the word of God? Let's look in:

1 Thes 4:17. *Then. we which are alive and remain shall be caught up together with them in the clouds to meet the Lord in the air.*

The actual Greek word for this phrase is "harpagisometha", and the Greek root is "harpazo". Vines dictionary defines "harpazo" this way, "to snatch or catch away." The next translation was to Latin. Which was "rapiemur", then we find the medieval Latin word "raptura" where we get the modern English word (rapture). Other meanings of this word are "to seize, to carry off, to catch up, to take away." In today's Christian world, this word "rapture" is the most commonly used word when referring to that time when Christ comes back to take His church home to heaven.

The Apostle Paul wrote in 1 Thessalonians 4:13-18 *But I would not have you to be ignorant, brethren, concerning them which are asleep, that ye sorrow not, even as others which have no hope. 14 For if we believe that Jesus died and rose again, even so them also which sleep in Jesus will God bring with him. 15 For this we say unto you by the word of the Lord, that we which are alive and remain unto the coming of the Lord shall not prevent them which are asleep. 16 For the Lord himself shall descend from heaven with a shout, with the voice of the archangel, and with the trump of God: and the dead in Christ shall rise first: 17 Then we which are alive and remain shall be caught up together with them in the clouds, to meet the Lord in the air: and so shall we ever be with the Lord. Wherefore comfort one another with these words.*

In 2 Peter 3:3-4, Peter says, *Scoffers will come in the last days, walking according t their own lusts, and saying, "Where is the promise of His coming? For since the fathers fell asleep, or literally died, all things continue as they were from the beginning of creation.*

So, they were saying, "There's no coming again of the Lord! It hasn't happened yet. It won't happen in the future." They were mocking the concept of the doctrine of the return of Jesus Christ. There will also be mockers in the last days, and those mockers have arrived!

As Christians, we believe in the incarnation, that God became a man in Christ; we believe in the crucifixion, that Jesus died on the cross for our sins; we believe in the Resurrection, that Jesus rose victoriously and bodily from the grave, we believe in the ascension, that Christ ascended back into heaven, and we believe in the exaltation, that Christ is seated at the right hand of God the Father. But, that's not the end of the story, we also believe in the return of Jesus Christ. He is coming again. As Christians, we focus so much on the birth of Jesus, His death and resurrection, but we forget that He is ascended, exalted and He will come again.

JESUS PROMISED TO COME AGAIN

John 14:2-3, Jesus said, *I go to prepare a place for you, and if I go and prepare a place for you, I will come again and receive you to myself, that where I am, there you may be also.*

As Christians we are called believers. Why? Because we believe His word. (The bible) If He promised that He is preparing a place and He promised that He would come to receive us (His Church) to Himself, that is a revelation of the rapture of the church. He said that He will take us to His Father's house. His promise will be fulfilled. This is the rapture of the Church!

We have scoffers, believers who do not believe that the rapture is a reality, some who do not believe that the rapture will take place before the tribulation, and some who believe that the rapture will take place when Jesus comes at the end of the tribulation, which means that the church would suffer through the agonizing events of the end time. Which is not scriptural.

THE PRE-TRIBULATION RAPTURE

It has become popular today to hear accusing sermons of those who believe in and teach on the pre-tribulation rapture. Their term used to describe those who believe what the Word of God teaches on the end time is "escapist who demotivate believers away from good works". In Titus 2:13, the Apostle Paul called the rapture *"Blessed hope and glorious appearing of our great God and Savior Jesus Christ.* We are called believers because we believe in the Lord and His word that promises a great escape from the wrath of God poured out in the seven year tribulation. The rapture will protect God's saints from the tribulation—between the rapture and the second coming (tribulation). Many are arguing that the tribulation period will begin before the rapture. But the bible says in Rom 8:1 That *there is therefore no condemnation to those who are in Christ Jesus.* Which suggests the church will not experience God's judgment during the Tribulation.

There are others who teach the church will go through part or all of the tribulation. But it is clear that God's wrath begins at the start of the tribulation when Jesus opens the seals and send for the four horsemen of the apocalypse after the rapture. In Paul's first epistle to the Thessalonians, he teaches on the topic of the rapture in every chapter and gives instruction for the church, *to wait for His Son from heaven, whom He raised from the dead, even Jesus who delivers us from the wrath to come.* (The tribulation.)

BIBLE PROOF OF THE PRE-TRIBULATION RAPTURE

1. Rev 9:11-21 Does not mention a resurrection.

This is the clearest picture of the second coming of Christ Jesus (The tribulation) But there is no mention of a resurrection where hundreds of millions of Christians will be resurrected and translated, yet there isn't any mention there. The rapture isn't mentioned because it doesn't happen at the second coming.

2. Zech 4:1-15 Doesn't mention a resurrection.
This is an Old Testament picture of Jesus returning to earth at the second coming. (The Tribulation) Still no mention of a resurrection.

3. Two different pictures are painted.
In the Old Testament there are two different pictures painted of the Messiah. One suffering (Isa 53:2-10, Psalm 22:6-8,11-18) and one reigning as King (Psalm 2:6-12, Zech 14:9,16.) As we look at these scriptures, we see they predicted two separate comings to the earth of the Messiah--the first coming as a suffering Messiah and the 2nd coming (still future) as a reigning King.

In the New Testament we have another picture added. Again, we have two pictures painted that don't look the same. These two different descriptions of Jesus' coming point to two separate events we call "The rapture" and the "second coming."

4. The known Day and the Unknown Day.
Concerning the return of Jesus, the Bible presents a day we can't know (Rapture) and a day we can know. Matt 25:13 says Jesus will return at an unknown time, while Rev 12:6 says the Jews will have to wait 1,260 days for the Lord to return. The 1,260 days begin when the Antichrist stands in the Temple and declares himself to be God (Matt 24:15-21, 2 Thes 2:4). The known and unknown days must happen at different times, meaning they are two separate events.

5. The elders have their crowns in heaven.

After John is called up into heaven, he sees the 24 elders with their rewards (crowns) Rev 4:4-10. We know that Christians will receive their rewards (crowns) at the rapture 2 Tim 4:8, Peter 5:4. We will be repaid at the resurrection of the righteous (Luke 14:14. The elders couldn't receive their crowns unless the resurrection (rapture has taken place.

6. The Holy ones are already with Jesus in heaven.

Zech 14:5,Rev 4:4-10. The armies in heaven, clothed in fine linen, follow Jesus out of heaven at His second coming (Rev 19:14, Zech 14:5, Col 3:4). These are not only angels because Rev 19:8 tells us the fine linen is the righteousness of the saints. In order to come out of heaven we first have to go in, indicating a previous rapture.

7. Raptured Saints are kept from the hour of testing.

Rev 3:10 *Because thou hast kept the word of my patience, I also will keep thee from the hour of temptation, which shall come upon all the world, to try them that dwell upon the earth.* Rev 3:10 Says we will be kept out of the hour of testing which will come upon the whole earth (The Tribulation). Some have wrongly believed "keep" means to keep through, or protect through the tribulation. Suppose you approach a high voltage area with a sign that says, "keep out."

Does that mean that you can enter and be protected? No, it means you are forbidden from entering the area. But this verse also says He will keep us from the hour of testing. It is not just the testing, but the time period. If a student is excused from a test, he still may have to sit in the class while others take the test. But if he is excused from the hour of testing, he can go home. The church will be called home before the hour of testing.

8. Angels don't resurrect people when they gather them for judgment.

When the angels are sent forth to gather the elect at the second coming (Matt 24:29-31) many have wrongly interpreted this as the rapture. The problem with this interpretation is, if we are resurrected at this time, why would we need angels to gather us? In the resurrection we will be like the angels (Matt 22:30), able to travel in the air at will. Obviously, these people who are gathered are not resurrected, therefore it can't be the rapture. No one would claim the wicked are raptured at this time, yet, Matt 13:39-41, 49 says the angels will not only gather the elect, but also the wicked. This gathering is not a resurrection.

9. Both the wicked and the righteous can't be taken first.

1 Thes 4:13-17 says the righteous are taken and the wicked are left behind, Matt 13:30 says the wicked are taken first and righteous are left behind. This points to two separate events, the rapture and the second coming.

10. Jesus will receive us to Himself, not us to receive Him

In John 14: 2-3 Jesus said He would prepare a place for the Church in heaven, then He would come again to receive us to Himself. Why would Jesus prepare a place for us in heaven and then not take us there? At the rapture, He will come to receive us to Himself, *"that where I am (heaven), there you may be also.* If the rapture took place at the same time as the second coming we would go up to the clouds and then immediately come back to the earth. That would contradict John 14:2-3.

11. The one who restrains is taken out of the way

In 2 Thes 2:6-7, Paul says *"The one who restrains will be taken out of the way.* We know that the Church is the biggest obstacle to the antichrist becoming a world ruler.

12. Who will populate the world in the Millennium?

If the rapture takes place at the second coming of Jesus and the wicked are cast into hell at that time, who will be left to populate the millennium? Only people in their natural (non-resurrected) bodies will be able to have children. Matt 22:30 For in the resurrection they neither marry, nor are given in marriage, but are as the angels of God in heaven. With a pre-tribulation rapture, the people saved after the rapture who are alive at the second coming will populate the earth during the millennium.

It will happen suddenly. There will be no prophetic word given pertaining to it's happening. Though if you are a child of God, (a believer), you should be expecting the rapture to take place at any time. The Lord did give us signs and events that would precede His return for His church. They have basically all manifested and are dictating the way the world is now operating. God's word is clear that Christ will come at a future point in time for those who belong to Him. Those who are the "dead in Christ" will experience their resurrection first and be gifted with glorified bodies when He comes. Those believers in Christ who are alive at that time will then be instantly transformed from their earthly state to their eternal state, and will not experience death. Instead, they will be caught up to meet the Lord in the air. Although we should be expecting to be raptured and shouldn't be surprised when it does happen, we don't know exactly when it will take place. After meeting with Christ in the air, we will head off to heaven to be with God the Father.

(1 Thes 5:1-9) *At the end of this age, on the day of Christ, we will see Christ coming in the air, believers living in this world will literally and suddenly be taken off this earth. The great power of God will take you off this planet to be with the Lord in heaven.*

What God purposed and predicted will definitely take place, and no one will have any power to stop, delay or change God's plan. *Of that day and hour no one knows, not even the angels of heaven, nor the Son of God, but the Father alone. (Matt 24:36)* The fact is that we are living in the last days and the rapture of the church is not far off and the end time birth pangs are getting more severe. The word of God gives us multitudes of events that will be occurring during the time before the rapture. The end time events are spelled out in God's word. We know that the time of the end is not known by anyone but God Himself, but He has given us His word that tells us of the events that will be taking place as we become closer and closer to the time of the rapture.

Signs of the Timing of the Rapture

Matt 24:36-44 *But of that day and hour knoweth no man, no, not the angels of heaven, but my Father only. 37 But as the days of Noe were, so shall also the coming of the Son of man be. 38 For as in the days that were before the flood they were eating and drinking, marrying and giving in marriage, until the day that Noe entered into the ark, 39 And knew not until the flood came, and took them all away; so shall also the coming of the Son of man be. 40 Then shall two be in the field; the one shall be taken, and the other left. 41 Two women shall be grinding at the mill; the one shall be taken, and the other left. 42 Watch therefore: for ye know not what hour your Lord doth come. 43 But know this, that if the good man of the house had known in what watch the thief would come, he would have watched, and would not have suffered his house to be broken up. 44 Therefore be ye also ready: for in such an hour as ye think not the Son of Man cometh.*

Just imagine, Jesus, sitting in the throne room beside the Father do not know when the rapture will take place. But God did give us a way that we can determine that the timing of the rapture is near by the end time events prophesied in His word taking place. In the lesson of the fig tree which was first explained to the disciples as they were leaving the Temple grounds in Jerusalem. They called the Lord's attention to the great buildings. Jesus replied that the day would come when not one stone of the Temple would be left standing upon another. The disciples were alarmed by Jesus' statement. So they asked Him, "*When will this happen? And what will be the sign of Your coming and the end of the age? (Church age)* Jesus did not give a time or date when these events would take place but told the disciples to learn the lesson from the fig tree.

Matt 24:32-33 *Now learn a parable of the fig tree; When his branch is yet tender, and putteth forth leaves, ye know that summer is nigh: 33 So likewise ye, when ye shall see all these things, know that it is near, even at the doors.*

The lesson from the Fig tree states that when we see the LEAVES begin to bud, we know that summer is soon to follow. With this simple lesson, the Lord explained how we can know the timing of an event. (The start of summer) based on where it falls in the order of events. (The start of summer comes after the blooming of the fig tree). Under the lesson from the Fig Tree, anticipating when an event is going to happen is simply a matter of watching for the events that must take place before the rapture of the church. What God purposed, planned and predicted will take place, and no one will have the power to stop it. When we accepted the Lord as our Savior, our citizenship changed. Heaven is now our home.

Phil 3:20-21 (Living) *But we are citizens of heaven, where the Lord Jesus Christ lives. And we are eagerly waiting for him to return as our Savior. 21 He will take our weak mortal bodies and change them into glorious bodies like his own, using the same power with which He will bring everything under his control.* So where are we at in the whole big scheme of things? We don't know exactly when the rapture will take place for, *of that day and hour no one knows, not even the angels of heaven, nor the Son, but the Father alone. (Matt24:36)* But we know that we are living in the end time and are in the beginning of birth pangs. This means that the coming of Christ to rapture the church is not far off. Heb 10:37 *For yet in a little while, He who is coming will come, and will not delay.* The word of God gives us many events that will take place before the rapture of the church. Here is a small list of them. What we are going through in our nation and in the world cannot be ignored or separated from the word of God in relation to the time that we are living in. As we look around in our cities, our states, our nation and the countries of the world, we see God's word manifesting before our very eyes.

Events That Will Take Place before the Rapture of the Church

During the end time the Bible says that wickedness and evil will run rampant all over the world. We can see that the world is being consumed with evil. In fact, sin has become so controlling that it is widely accepted even though the activities are clearly forbidden in the bible. Let's look at what the word of God says about end time evil of the last days.

Matt 24:3-15 *And as he sat upon the Mount of Olives, the disciples came unto him privately, saying, Tell us, when shall these things be? and what shall be the sign of thy coming, and of the end of the world? 4nd Jesus answered and said unto them, Take heed that no man deceive you.* (With actions and events) *For many shall come in my name, saying, I am Christ; and shall deceive many. 6 And ye shall hear of wars and rumors of wars: see that ye be not troubled: for all these things must come to pass, but the end is not yet. 7 For nation shall rise against nation, and kingdom against kingdom: and there shall be famines, and pestilences, and earthquakes in divers places. 8 All these are the beginning of sorrows.* (Not just pre-rapture, but increasing into the tribulation) *9 Then shall they deliver you up to be afflicted, and shall kill you: and ye shall be hated of all nations for my name's sake. 10 And then shall many be offended, and shall betray one another, and shall hate one another. 11*

And many false prophets shall rise, and shall deceive many. 12 And because iniquity shall abound, the love of many shall wax cold. 13 But he that shall endure unto the end, the same shall be saved. (This is definitely the signs that we're seeing today) *And this gospel of the kingdom shall be preached in all the world for a witness unto all nations; and then shall the end come.*

2 Tim 3:1-5 *This know also, that in the last days perilous times shall come. 2 For men shall be lovers of their own selves, covetous, boasters, proud, blasphemers, disobedient to parents, unthankful, unholy, 3 Without natural affection, trucebreakers, false accusers, incontinent, fierce, despisers of those that are good, 4 Traitors, heady, high minded, lovers of pleasures more than lovers of God; 5 Having a form of godliness, but denying the power thereof: from such turn away.*

We not only have an increase of wickedness and evil in our nation and the world, but we have a great increase in violence, pride, arrogance, liberalism, homosexuality, abortion and religious compromise. This end time evil was warned by Jesus and as God's children of Israel resist, the world will hate them and many will abandon their Christian faith. When you study the subject of the rapture of the church, you will see that there's so much more that takes place during that time. The Lord Jesus said that no one knew the date, time or hour of His return to the earth but God the Father. (Matt 24:36) But He did say that we could discern the signs of the times and realize the time is near. (Luke 21:24-28). These are some of the signs that Christians world-wide should be aware of.

Matt 24:33 *So likewise ye, when ye shall see all these things, know that the end is near, even at the door.*

THE REGATHERING OF ISRAEL

The destruction of Israel began in 70 AD by the Roman Empire and continued until Hitler's reign of terror ended. In 1945, the nation had ceased to exist, and the Jewish people were dispersed throughout the world. In 1948 the Jewish people from all parts of the world returned to their homeland and the nation of Israel was reborn, in fulfillment of God's prophetic word.

Amos 9:14-15 *And I will bring again the captivity of my people of Israel, and they shall build the waste cities, and inhabit them; and they shall plant vineyards, and drink the wine thereof; they shall also make gardens, and eat the fruit of them. 15 And I will plant them upon their land, and they shall no more be pulled up out of their land which I have given them, saith the Lord thy God.*

This return of the Jewish people to their homeland is a foreshadow of a greater return that will take place at the end of the tribulation. In 1967 in the six-day war, The Jews took control of Jerusalem for the first time in many centuries. And finally in 2018, Jerusalem became the capital city of Israel. Remember this is just a foreshadow of what will be experienced during the tribulation after the rapture of the Church. According to the word of God the man that arise to power over the nations after the rapture will be the one that is the Anti-Christ who will form some sort of peace pact with Israel at the start of the tribulation, and have something to do with the construction of a new temple for worship. (more on this coming). Many of the Jews will accept this man as the long awaited Messiah, until midway through the tribulation period at which time he will set up an image of himself in the Holy of Holies, proclaim that he is God and demand that He and the images be worshiped at which time their rejection will bring great persecution and the destruction prophesied in God's word. (The abomination of desolation. (Mark 13:14)

Knowledge Is Increased

In the last 100 years man has gone from horse and buggy, to the moon. In the last 50 years there has been an explosion of new technology, bringing the whole world together, making almost all things possible for sinful man to destroy himself and the nations with weapons of mass destruction. There are nations who hold weapons that can destroy nations without a major army. With the separation and hostility that is permeating the nations, it is basically a threat to all nations. The age of the personal computer has given the individual access to the world. This technology has made it easier for man to cover the earth with evil and hatred.

Signs in Man

When you turn the TV on you see the scriptures being fulfilled, as we are being bombarded by sin being exploited and it's acceptance as entertainment or natural. Television's destruction of Christian faith by promoting homosexuality, abortion, sexual permissiveness, and applauds anyone who supports their ungodliness. Our schools have become killing fields, infested with drugs and disrespect for God's word and the Church.

A. Scoffers

There are those who have spiritual authority, called by God to prepare His people for the rapture, but they are denying the reality of the rapture. Then there are those who do not know the Lord, but denies the reality of what His word says is going to take place. Then there are those who believe that the rapture will take place during the tribulation and not before it. We will look at the terrible activity that will take place during the tribulation and how few people will escape hell when it ends.

2 Peter 3:2-3 *Knowing this first, that there shall come in the last days scoffers, walking after their own lusts, 3 And saying, Where is the promise of His coming? For since the fathers fell asleep, all things continue as they were from the beginning of creation.*

B. Homosexuality

Rom 1:25-28 *Who changed the truth of God into a lie, and worshiped and served the creature more than the Creator, who is blessed forever. Amen. 26 For this cause God gave them up unto vile affections: for even their women did change the natural use into that which is against nature: 27 And likewise also the men, leaving the natural use of the woman, burned in their lust one toward another; men with men working that which is unseemly, and receiving in themselves that recompence of their error which was meet. 32 Who knowing the judgement of God, that they who commit such things are worthy of death, not only do the sane but have pleasure in them that do them.*

Homosexuality has been around since the dawn of time but never before in all of history has it been flaunted and embraced with such enthusiasm by society. It has been dressed up as in the clothing of an alternate lifestyle and passed off to society as normal. But God says that it is an abomination and will reap its reward.

C. Lovers of Self

2 Tim 3:1-5 *This know also, that in the last days perilous times shall come. 2 For men shall be lovers of their own selves, covetous, boasters, proud, blasphemers, disobedient to parents, unthankful, unholy, 3 Without natural affection, trucebreakers, false accusers, incontinent, fierce, despisers of those that are good, 4 Traitors, heady, high minded, lovers of pleasures more than lovers of God; 5 Having a form of godliness, but denying the power thereof: from such turn away.*

For the purpose of selfish ambition, careers and lack of personal responsibility, expecting mothers abort their unborn children, depriving them of a chance at life. Driven by lust, and a few disgusting moments of personal satisfaction, a man will rape and murder a child. The terrible list goes on and on. When self reigns, what God wants doesn't seem to matter, no matter how much calamity it causes in the earth. Without God, man is lost in a downward spiral and will end up in the terrible tribulation.

D. Iniquity Abounding

Matt 24:12 *And because iniquity shall abound, the love of many shall grow cold.*

Hatred, violence and rage is controlling many, causing murders, prejudice, anger and criminal activity. Unfortunately, it is being minimized in its seriousness and not penalized as it was in the past.

E. Cults and the Occult Abounding

Matt 24:4-6 *And Jesus answered and said unto them, Take heed that no man deceive you .5 For many shall come in my name, saying, I am Christ; and shall deceive many.* Matt 24:11 *And many false prophets shall rise, and shall deceive many.*

Matt 24:24 *For there shall arise false Christs, and false prophets, and shall shew great signs and wonders; insomuch that, if it were possible, they shall deceive the very elect.*

Have you noticed the renewed and greater interest in occult practices? Almost in every city you can find advertisements for palm and tarot card readings, physic predictions, and connections to other occultic practices. Even the churches are getting involved. the newspapers are carrying ads promoting occultic entertainment. And online occultic activities are rampant. It is considered as entertainment on television.

F. Warfare

Mark 13:7-8 *And when ye shall hear of wars and rumors of wars, be ye not troubled: for such things must needs be; but the end shall not be yet. 8 For nation shall rise against nation, and kingdom against kingdom: and there shall be earthquakes in divers places, and there shall be famines and troubles: these are the beginnings of sorrows.*

Matt 24:7-8 *For nation shall rise against nation, and kingdom against kingdom: and there shall be famines, and pestilences, and earthquakes, in divers places. 8 All these are the beginning of sorrows.*

We have not only seen two world wars, but nation against nation. We are now in a period where the threat of war is permeating over the whole world. In the last thirty years we have not been able to go on the news without hearing of a major war some place on the face of the earth. It is the buildup for the great world war that is presented to us in the scriptures, referred to in Rev 16 as the battle of Armageddon with Jesus prevailing.

For nation shall rise against nation, and kingdom against kingdom: and there shall be famines, and pestilences, and earthquakes, in divers places.

SIGNS IN THE CHURCH

A. Apostacy

2 Thes 2:3 *Let no man deceive you by any means, for that day shall not come. except there come a falling away first, and that man of sin be revealed.*

1 Tim 4:1 *Now the Spirit speaks expressly, that in the latter times some shall depart from the faith, giving heed to seducing spirits and doctrines of devils.*

1 Tim 4:3-4 *For the time will come when they will not endure sound doctrine; but after their own lusts shall they heap to themselves teachers, having itching ears; 4 And*

shall turn away their ears from the truth, and shall be turned into fables.

Apostacy means falling away. One must fall away from something to something. There are many who have fallen away from the foundational truths that Christians have embraced and held dear to for centuries. Many have departed from faith in Jesus Christ and have accepted a false gospel. We have only seen the beginning of this falling away that the word of God tells us is going to take place.

B. The Gospel Preached Worldwide

Matt 24:14 *And this gospel of the kingdom shall be preached in all the world for a witness unto all nations; and then shall the end come.*

With all the communication technology that exists today, the gospel has been preached worldwide, or is close to it. Although multitudes will reject the gospel after hearing God's offering of eternal life in heaven, it will not affect God's rapturing those who accept His offering of eternal life.

Our Lord Jesus Christ is alive in Heaven and He is coming back on that glorious rapture day. We, God's Church must be ready always for His blessed return for His children because it will happen suddenly and unexpectedly whether Rapture scoffers, lukewarm believers and those who are not believers deny the reality of the imminent rapture or not. We must always be ready for the appearing of our Savior, Jesus Christ, because it is a biblical and prophetic event.

1 Cor 15:51-52 *Behold, I shew you a mystery; We shall not all sleep, but we shall all be changed, 52 In a moment, in the twinkling of an eye, at the last trump: for the trumpet shall sound, and the dead shall be raised incorruptible, and we shall be changed.*

1 Thes 4:16-17 *For the Lord himself shall descend from heaven with a shout, with the voice of the archangel, and with the trump of God: and the dead in Christ shall rise first: 17 Then we which are alive and remain shall be caught up together with them in the clouds, to meet the Lord in the air: and so shall we ever be with the Lord.*

The word tells us that no one can know the day or the hour of the rapture. (Matt 24:36, Mark 13:32-33; Luke 21:34-35). Those professing to know the day or the hour are deceiving themselves. The rapture will occur suddenly and unexpectedly. Many wonder why it is taking so long for the rapture to take place. We must not be afraid but stay in expectancy of the glorious appearance of our Lord and Savior Jesus Christ! Pre-tribulation rapture is a reality and our blessed hope. Jesus gave us the pre-tribulation rapture divine assurance in the bible:

Rev 3:10 *Because you have kept My command to persevere, I (Lord Jesus Christ) also will keep you from the hour of trial (7 years worldwide Tribulation period) which shall come upon the whole world, to test those who dwell on earth. (After the church is raptured).*

THE JUDGEMENT SEAT OF CHRIST

2 Tim 4:7-8 *I have fought a good fight, I have finished my course, I have kept the faith: 8 Henceforth there is laid up for me a crown of righteousness, which the Lord, the righteous judge, shall give me at that day: and not to me only, but unto all them also that love His appearing.*

As a born again Christian, we must be getting ready for the glorious rapture, but are we aware that we will have to give account of our service for our Lord Jesus Christ while we were on earth? We must understand that this is not a judgement that will determine heaven or hell. After we are raptured, hell is out of the picture for us. But this is what will take place in heaven after we are raptured, the judgement seat of Christ after our entrance into heaven. There will be given to God's children, a CROWN OF RIGHTEOUSNESS which will be placed on the heads of all of God's dedicated raptured children by Jesus Christ. The Judgment Seat of Christ is not a final exam to determine our suitability for heaven. If we have trusted Jesus as our Savior, our sins have been forgiven, and that is what qualifies us to enter the holy presence of God in heaven. The Word of God tells us that "*There is no condemnation to those who are in Jesus Christ.* (Romans 8:1) Our sins were all paid for on Calvery's cross.

When we stand before the Judgment Seat of Christ, our faithful service to Him will be evaluated and rewarded. Some of the things we might be judged on are how well we obeyed the Great Commission (Matt 28:18-20, How faithfully we served Lord Jesus Christ (1 Cor 9:4-27; 2 Tim 2:5). With His knowledge of all things, He will assess our every thought, motive, and action. With understanding of this judgement, we should be motivated to be more like Christ Jesus in our daily life, running our spiritual race towards His heavenly rewards.

1 .Cor 9:24-25 *Know ye not that they which run in a race run all, but one receiveth the prize? So run, that ye may obtain. 25 And every man that striveth for the mastery is temperate in all things. Now they do it to obtain a corruptible crown; but we an incorruptible crown.*

The bible speaks of born again believers receiving crowns for different things based on how faithfully they served the Lord. There are five Heavenly Crowns mentioned in the New Testament that will be awarded to believers. They are, the Imperishable crown, the crown of rejoicing, the crown of righteousness, the crown of glory and the crown of life. In the New Testament this word crown is used to speak of the rewards of Heaven that God promises to the those who faithfully served the Lord Jesus Christ.

THE CROWN OF RIGHTEOUSNESS: All those raptured will get the crown of righteousness because they were ready for His glorious appearance. The crown of righteousness will be the reward for perpetual watchfulness, as we eagerly love, watch and await His glorious appearance in the sky.

There will also be awarded the CROWN OF REJOICING for active soul-winners for the Lord.

I Thes 2:19-20 *For what is our hope, or joy, or crown of rejoicing? Are not even ye in the presence of our Lord Jesus Christ at his coming? 20 For ye are our glory and joy.*

There will also be awarded AN INCORRUPTIBLE CROWN for overcoming the old nature. 1 Cor 9:25-27

There will be awarded a CROWN OF LIFE for enduring persecution and trials while on earth. James 1:12, Rev 2:10

There will be awarded the CROWN OF GLORY for shepherding the flock of Christ. This crown of glory is a special crown that will be awarded by the Lord Jesus Christ to dedicated men and women of God who share or teaches the Word of God . (The Bible) They could be Evangelists, Pastors, Ministers of the word, Sunday School Teachers or anyone who teaches the Word of God faithfully to others. Rom 14:10-12 says, *For we will all stand before God's judgment seat…So then, each of us will give an account of himself to God*

As we stand before the Judgment Seat of Christ for decoration, each raptured Saint will already be wearing a shining garment (Rev. 19:8). The heavenly garment will be made of linen, white and clean. Before the decorations can be distributed individually, the works of all raptured saints will be tested. One by one, we will be summoned and an angel will bring a very huge package containing all the works that we have done from the day we were born-again until the day the Lord raptures His Church. Everything we did before we were born-again are already forgotten, the blood of Jesus cleanses from all sins (1 John 1:7. When the angel brings the package, there will be ready a divine fire of assessment burning and that package will be thrown into the fire which continue to burn.

1 Cor 3:11-15 *For other foundation can no man lay than that is laid, which is Jesus Christ. 12 Now if any man build upon this foundation gold, silver, precious stones, wood, hay, stubble; 13 Every man's work shall be made manifest: for the day shall declare it, because it shall be revealed by fire; and the fire shall try every man's work of what sort it is. 14 If any man's work abide which he hath built thereupon, he shall receive a reward. 15 If any man's work shall be burned, he shall suffer loss: but he himself shall be saved; yet so as by fire.*

A major reason that will make so many works burn is the motive behind the works we are doing for the Lord. Some people give to the Gospel because they want to be seen. You can be certain that everything you give so that you can be seen is going to be burnt on that day. Some people work for the Lord because they want to be known. The work done with that kind of motive is going to be burnt. Your motive for working hard for the Lord is to walk in obedience to Him and win souls for the Lord Jesus Christ is because of your love for Him.

1 Cor 15:58 *Therefore, my beloved brethren, be ye steadfast, unmovable, always abounding in the work of the Lord, for as much as ye know that your labor is not in vain in the Lord.*

Our reward is in heaven for everything we do on earth for Christ's sake. Our treasure is in heaven. Our selfless service for our Lord Jesus Christ will be bountifully rewarded in heaven at the Judgment Seat of Christ.

Rom 14:10-12 *But why dost thou judge thy brother? or why dost thou set at nought thy brother? for we shall all stand before the judgment seat of Christ. 11 For it is written, As I live, saith the Lord, every knee shall bow to me, and every tongue shall confess to God. 12 So then everyone of us shall give account of himself to God.*

You will not take to heaven on imminent glorious rapture day anything you have acquired on this sinful earth. You will only ascend to Heaven on rapture day as a glorious Saint in your glorious white garment of righteousness. (Rev 19:8, 14) We must make sure that we're utilizing our divine call, time, talents and God given resources to touch lives in this grace period while awaiting the glorious rapture. Everything we are doing for our Lord Jesus Christ should be done because of our love for Him and our desire to glorify Him. Being a spectator Christian does not glorify the Lord or cause others to come into the Kingdom of God. Our service to the Lord in this life will determine what our service will be during the 1000 year reign of Christ during the Millennial Reign.

EFFECTS OF THE RAPTURE UPON CHRISTIANS WHO ARE IN HEAVEN

1. YOU WILL BE WITH JESUS AND WILL REMAIN WITH HIM.

This is the best and most heart stirring aspect of the rapture, that He's coming for us. That He wants you to be with Him, that you will see Him, that He will express His love for you, that you will express your love to Him, and then forever be with Him, your Redeemer and Lord.

John 17:24 *Father, I will that they also, whom thou hast given me, be with me where I am; that they may behold my glory, which thou hast given me: for thou lovest me before the foundation of the world.*

2. YOU WILL BE REDEEMED.

You will be released from this wicked world, delivered and taken out of this evil and rebellious place. But not only that, your soul will be redeemed. You will be given a heavenly body.

3. YOU WILL BE GLORIFIED.

You will be given a brand new body—a Heavenly body! It will be a powerful, spiritual, and immortal body, one that will last for eternity. Your salvation will finally be complete. Having been justified and sanctified on earth, you will be glorified as you leave the earth to be with Jesus.

4. YOU WILL BE GREATLY REJOICING IN HEAVEN.

You will be wholeheartedly focused on the lord, praising and thanking Him for your salvation, thanking Him for His love for you.

Rev 7:9 *They cry out with a loud voice, saying, "Salvation to our God who sits on the throne, and to the Lamb.*

5. YOU WILL BE RICHLY REWARDED

for your labor for God. This reward is just the beginning of a glorious inheritance that you will experience for all eternity. The reward of God's blessings for His children who have loved Him and served Him during their time on earth.

7. YOU WILL REST FROM YOUR LABORS.

Life is becoming difficult on earth. Even if you are working for the Lord, sacrificing and suffering for Him as evil is permeating the earth. The Lord's servants will be under attack by Satan and tired, but then you will rest and be lifted up when Jesus Christ returns and you are raptured from the earth.

8. YOU WILL BE GATHERED TOGETHER.

You will be assembled and joined together with other believers and taken to be with Jesus Christ. Believers from all time, those who have already died and gone to heaven, and those who were still alive on earth will be gathered together.

Phil 3:20-21 *For our conversation is in heaven; from whence also we look for the Saviour, the Lord Jesus Christ: 21 Who shall change our vile body, that it may be fashioned like unto his glorious body, according to the working whereby He is able even to subdue all things unto himself.*

9. YOU WILL BE REUNITED WITH BELIEVING LOVED ONES.

Those who have already died and gone on before you. You will be with other believers you had heard about or read about in God's word. This will be a glorious gathering, with a multitude of believers celebrating together, loving one another and worshiping the Lord.

Rev 7:9-10 *After this I beheld, and, lo, a great multitude, which no man could number, of all nations, and kindreds, and people, and tongues, stood before the throne, and before the Lamb, clothed with white robes, and palms in their hands;10 And cried with a loud voice, saying, Salvation to our God which sitteth upon the throne, and unto the Lamb.*

2 Cor 5:10 *For we must all appear before the judgment seat of Christ; that every one may receive the things done in his body, according to that he hath done, whether it be good or bad.*

THE CHOICE IS OURS, GO OR STAY!

Our Lord and Savior Jesus Christ is alive in heaven and He is coming back on the glorious rapture day. We must be ready always because it is a biblical and prophetic event.

Mark 13:32-37 *But of that day and that hour knoweth no man, no, not the angels which are in heaven, neither the Son, but the Father. 33 Take ye heed, watch and pray: for ye know not when the time is. 34 For the Son of man is as a man taking a far journey, who left his house, and gave authority to his servants, and to every man his work, and commanded the porter to watch. 35 Watch ye therefore: for ye know not when the master of the house cometh, at even, or at midnight, or at the cockcrowing, or in the morning: 36 Lest coming suddenly he find you sleeping. 37 And what I say unto you I say unto all, Watch.*

No one know when the rapture will take place, it doesn't matter how spiritual you are. If Jesus who sits beside our almighty God doesn't know, why would God reveal the time to struggling Christians on earth? So, rapture date setting is futile. Remember the word tells us that in the last days false prophets would be among us. Rapture date setters are not only deceiving themselves, but they are deceiving others. We must be led by the Lord and His Word. The glorious rapture will occur suddenly and unexpectedly! It is true that the rapture seems to be overdue but we must never give up staying prepared for the coming of the Lord. He has delayed the rapture for over 2000 years. Why? Because He is a merciful God, who desires to save multitudes of souls worldwide. Suppose the rapture had taken place the day before you gave your heart to the Lord. Where would you be? We must never give up our blessed hope because it will happen suddenly and unexpectedly whether rapture scoffers, lukewarm believers and unbelievers believe it or not. There are many that mock and laugh at those who believe in the rapture and the tribulation. They laugh at the whole idea of the end of the world and the judgment of Christ. II Peter 3:3 *Knowing this first, that there shall come in the last days scoffers, walking after their own lusts*. WE MUST STAY READY!

Titus 2:13-14 Looking for that blessed hope, and the glorious appearing of the great God and our Saviour, Jesus Christ; 14 Who gave himself for us, that he might redeem us from all iniquity, and purify unto himself a peculiar people, zealous of good work.

There is much that we do not know about the events that will take place before, during and after the rapture, but the word of God tells us to *have faith in God!* We must not be afraid to be moved into the presence of God. We know that God's word is true. What He said will be happening after the rapture of the churches is already being prepared for the tribulation period.

The Great Tribulation period will begin when we the church is translated (raptured) to meet the Lord in the air. The Church must be ready! The tribulation will bring upon this world horrors, destruction, pain and terrorism that have never been seen or imagined upon this earth. We must be ready when the Lord raptures His Church. Those who miss the rapture will experience the terrible seven years of tribulation. This is a time of Satan's attempted takeover of the earth. But God's word tells us that God has already taken care of this through the tribulation victory. VICTORY IN JESUS! The terrible thing is that billions who will not be raptured will be involved in the horrors of the tribulation without good endings.

CAUSE OF THE TRIBULATION MAN'S REBELLION

Although God is totally holy and sin is abhorring to Him, as well as a lost humanity; God because of His great love for His creation and not willing that any of us perish/; gave His only begotten Son (Jesus Christ) that whoever believes in Jesus could have eternal life and a relationship with God. The wrath of God will be poured out during the tribulation period upon this earth because of man's unrepentant heart and rejection of God's gift. Again, the tribulation will bring to the earth such horrible events the world has not seen or experienced before.

THE WORD "TRIBULATION" MEANS: As listed in the *Merriam-Webster* dictionary, "tribulation" means distress or suffering resulting from oppression or persecution. According to *Easton's Bible Dictionary*, tribulation is trouble or affliction of any kind. "Tribulation and anguish" are the corrective sufferings that shall overtake the wicked.

Matt. 24:21: *For then shall be great tribulation, such as was not since the beginning of the world to this time, no, nor ever shall be.* The word indicates the trials to accompany Jerusalem's destruction.

The word "tribulation" is used to describe any kind of testing, affliction, or distress. In the Bible, the term "tribulation" refers to a specific eschatological time of trouble. After the rapture of the Church, a special time of judgement from God that will last seven years will impact the entire world. This will be a time of unprecedented affliction and will culminate in the return of Jesus Christ. The word "tribulation" is used to describe any kind of testing, affliction, or distress that people experience throughout life. In the Bible, the term "tribulation" refers to a specific eschatological time of trial, testing, and trouble. This will be a special time of judgement from God that will impact the entire world and will be unprecedented in its affliction. All this will culminate in the return of Jesus Christ and the end of Satan's existence on earth and His eternal existence in hell.

Matt. 24:29–36: *Immediately after the tribulation of those days shall the sun be darkened, and the moon shall not give her light, and the stars shall fall from heaven, and the powers of the heavens shall be shaken: 30 And then shall appear the sign of the Son of man in heaven: and then shall all the tribes of the earth mourn, and they shall see the Son of man coming in the clouds of heaven with power and great glory. 31 And he shall send his angels with a great sound of a trumpet, and they shall gather together his elect from the four winds, from one end of heaven to the other. 32 Now learn a parable of the fig tree; When his branch is yet tender, and putteth forth leaves, ye know that summer is nigh: 33 So likewise ye, when ye shall see all these things, know that it is near, even at the doors. 34 Verily I say unto you, This generation shall not pass, till all these things be fulfilled. 35 Heaven and earth shall pass away, but my words shall not pass away. 36 But of that day and hour knoweth no man, no, not the angels of heaven, but my Father only.*

The Day of the Lord

Isa. 2:12: *For the day of the LORD of hosts shall be upon every one that is proud and lofty, and upon every one that is lifted up; and he shall be brought low.*

Isa. 13:6: *Wail, for the day of the LORD is at hand! It will come as destruction from the Almighty* (NKJ).

Isa. 13:9: *Behold, the day of the LORD comes, Cruel, with both wrath and fierce anger, To lay the land desolate; And He will destroy its sinners from it* (NKJ).

The tribulation encompasses a future seven-year period when God will complete his discipline of Israel and final judgment upon the unbelieving citizens of the world. Christians who have trusted Christ as Lord and Savior will escape the tribulation.

The Final Seven-Year Period of Daniel's "Seventy Weeks"

Dan. 9:24–2: *Seventy "sevens" are decreed for your people and your holy city to finish transgression, to put an end to sin, to atone for wickedness, to bring in everlasting righteousness, to seal up vision and prophecy and to anoint the most holy. Know and understand this: From the issuing of the decree to restore and rebuild Jerusalem until the Anointed One, the ruler, comes, there will be seven "sevens," and sixty-two "sevens." It will be rebuilt with streets and a trench, but in times of trouble. After the sixty-two "sevens," the Anointed One will be cut off and will have nothing. The people of the ruler who will come will destroy the city and the sanctuary. The end will come like a flood: War will continue until the end, and desolations have been decreed. He will confirm a covenant with many for one "seven." In the middle of the "seven," he will put an end to sacrifice and offering. And on a wing of the temple, he will set up an abomination that causes desolation, until the end that is decreed is poured out on him* (NIV). The "great tribulation" refers to the second half of the seven-year period.

Matt. 24:21: *For then shall be great tribulation, such as was not since the beginning of the world to this time, no, nor ever shall be.*

Zeph. 1:15: *That day will be a day of wrath, a day of distress and anguish, a day of trouble and ruin, a day of darkness and gloom, a day of clouds and blackness.*

THE BEGINNING OF THE TRIBULATION

The tribulation period here on earth will begin when the church is raptured to meet the Lord in the air. But those whom Satan will use are revealed after the rapture in the midst of a warring world and a designated attack on Israel and other nations that offered support to God's chosen nation. This man, as the leader of a federation of ten nations, basically will be in control of the world, politically. This will encompass a seven-year period; during the first three and a half years of the seven-year tribulation, who he is will be revealed.

THE RISE OF THE ANTICHRIST

Rev. 1 3:1–10: *And I stood upon the sand of the sea, and saw a great beast rise up out of the sea, having seven heads and ten horns, and upon his horns ten crowns, and upon his heads the name of blasphemy.*

Dan. 7:8: Called the Little Horn

Dan. 9:26: Called the prince that shall come

2 Thes 2:3 Called the man of sin

Called the beast out of the sea

This man, the antichrist, will be controlled and influenced by Satan himself. He will seem to have all the solutions for the Middle East problems. He will make a seven year peace treaty with Israel and have a new temple built and will be the leader of the one world government during the tribulation. Remember, there is no active church left on earth after the rapture, and those who were professing to be the church and living like the world are no longer the church. The church is in heaven after the rapture! This man who seem to be in control of the earth will be supported by the false prophet who will rise to power over the world religions. (Without Jesus or God)

THE RISE OF THE FALSE PROPHET

The false prophet will rise to power as head over the false religions system that is left upon the earth after the church is raptured. As the second beast of Rev 13, he will declare that the antichrist is the Messiah, will demand that people worship him and cause people to receive his mark on their foreheads or right hand.

Rev. 13:11-13 *And I beheld another beast coming up out of the earth; and he had two horns like a lamb, and he spake as a dragon. 12 and he exerciseth all the power of the first beast before him, and causeth the earth and them which dwell therein to worship the first beast, whose deadly wound was healed. 13 and he doeth great wonders, so that he maketh fire come down from heaven on the earth in the sight of men.* (Read Rev vs 14-18.)

THE SEALING OF 144,000 JEWS

Twelve thousand Jews from each of the 12 tribes of Israel will be set apart for God's service during the tribulation period. These servants of God, will have God's seal in their foreheads; These 144,000 will preach the gospel worldwide until they are killed during the tribulation causing multitudes to repent and receive the Lord as their Savior.

Rev 7:3 *Hurt not the earth, neither the sea, nor the trees, till we have sealed the servants of God in their foreheads.*

Rev 14:1 *And I looked and, lo, a Lamb stood on the Mount Zion, and with him an hundred forty and four thousand, having his Father's name written in their forehead.*

THE TWO WITNESSES

Rev 11:3 *And I will give power unto my two witnesses and they shall prophesy a thousand two hundred and threescore days, clothed in sackcloth.*

The ministry of these two men will be the first three and a half years of the seven year tribulation. (Many believe that they are Elijah and Enoch because God took them to heaven before they died a physical death.) To validate the prophesies of these two men, God grants miraculous signs and miracles by their hands. (V 5-6). The 144,000 Jewish Evangelist were saved because of these two miracle working servants of God who were eventually killed, but God raised them from the dead after three days.

THE WRATH OF GOD POURED OUT

The wrath of God will be poured out during the tribulation period upon this earth because of man's unrepentant heart and rejection of God's gift. Within the opening of the 7 seals, the 7 trumpets and the 7 vials, God's wrath is revealed. This will be the worst time ever or ever could be on earth or heaven. It is estimated that at least two thirds of the population will not survive the tribulation. This should not be a surprise, God has been merciful during over two thousand years after Jesus came to the earth and paid the price for the sins of those who would accept His forgiveness. All of those on earth during these seven years of tribulation did not accept God's gift of salvation from the tribulation. Or perhaps they accepted the gift of salvation but walked away from the gift of eternal life with God as many are doing today.

The Seven Seals Judgement

Rev 6:1-17 The opening of the first 6 seals which contain this information.

Seal 1: Rev 6:2 *And I saw, and behold a white horse; and he that sat upon him had a bow; and a crown was given to him; and he went forth conquering and to conquer.* (The false prophet or the anti-christ).

Seal 2: Rev 6:3-4 *And when he had opened the second seal, I heard the second beast say come and see. 4 And there went out another horse that was red, and power was given to him that sat thereon to take peace from the earth, and that they should kill one another: and there was given to him a great sword.*
This person's influence will be the result of world war.

Seal 3: Rev 6:5-6 *And when he had opened the third seal, I heard the third beast say, come and see. And I beheld, and lo a black horse, and he that sat on him had a pair of balances in his hand. 6 And I heard a voice in the midst of the four beasts say, A measure of wheat for a penny; and see thou hurt not the oil and the wine.*
The opening of this seal brings about a worldwide economic crisis.

Seal 4: Rev 6:7-8 *And when he had opened the. fourth seal, I heard the voice of the fourth beast say, come and see. 8 And I looked, and behold a pale horse; and his name that sat upon him was death and Hell followed with him. And power was given unto them over the fourth part of the earth, to kill with sword and with hunger, and with death, and with the beasts of the earth.*

Global starvation, war and death will follow the opening of the fourth seal.

Seal 5: Rev 6:9-11 *And when he had opened the fifth seal, I saw under the altar the souls of them that were slain for the word of God, and for the testimony which they held: 10 And they cried with a loud voice, saying, How long, O Lord, holy and true, dost thou not judge and avenge our blood on them that dwell on the earth? 11 And white robes were given unto every one of them; and it was said unto them, that they should rest yet for a little season, until their fellow servants also and their brethren, that should be killed as they were, should be fulfilled.*

As the result of the chosen 144,000 Jews, many will turn to Jesus; who will be persecuted for their faith and refusal to bow to the antichrist and receive his mark and will be tortured and slain.

Seal 6: Rev 6:12-*17 And I beheld when he had opened the sixth seal, and, lo, there was a great earthquake; and the sun became black as sackcloth of hair, and the moon became as blood; 13 And the stars of heaven fell unto the earth, even as a fig tree casteth her untimely figs, when she is shaken of a mighty wind. 14 And the heaven departed as a scroll when it is rolled together; and every mountain and island were moved out of their places. 15 And the kings of the earth, and the great men, and the rich men, and the chief captains, and the mighty men, and every bondman, and every free man, hid themselves in the dens and in the rocks of the mountains; 16 And said to the mountains and rocks, Fall on us, and hide us from the face of him that sitteth on the throne, and from the wrath of the Lamb: 17 For the great day of his wrath is come; and who shall be able to stand?*

Whatever takes place with the opening of this seal, it effects the sun, moon and earth to the point, that people hide in fear.

Seal 7: There is a lull in judgment between the 6th and 7th seal as God gives people time to repent. The opening of the 7th seal (Rev 8:1-2) is the releasing of the 7 trumpets judgments.

The Seven Trumpet Judgements

Trumpet 1: Rev 8:6-7 *And the seven angels which had the seven trumpets prepared themselves to sound. 7 The first angel sounded, and there followed hail and fire mingled with blood, and they were cast upon the earth: and the third part of trees was burnt up, and all green grass was burnt up.*

All these things that are taking place are the results of the rejection of God's love and His plans for the earth and His creation. Satan's plan will not prevail. God is still in charge of the world.

Trumpet 2: Rev 8:8-9 *And the second angel sounded, and as it were a great mountain burning with fire was cast into the sea: and the third part of the sea became blood; 9 And the third part of the creatures which were in the sea, and had life, died; and the third part of the ships were destroyed.*

The supernatural hand of God moves in the midst of rebellion against His word and His people. The tribulation is the result of the rejection of Almighty God. Remember in the Old Testament God rained down plagues upon Egypt.

Trumpet 3: Rev 8:10-11 *And the third angel sounded, and there fell a great star from heaven, burning as if it was a lamp, and it fell upon the third part of the rivers, and upon the fountains of the waters.* 11 *And the name of the star is called Wormwood: and the third part of the waters became wormwood; and many men died of the waters, because they were made bitter.*

That star is what we call a meteorite.

Trumpet 4: Rev 8:12 *And the fourth angel sounded and the third part of the sun was smitten, and the third part of the moon, and the third part of the stars; so as the third part of them was darkened and the day shone not for a thirdpart of it, and the night likewise.* (Read verse 13)

Trumpet 5: Rev 9:1-3 And the fifth angel sounded, and I saw a star fall from heaven unto the earth: and to him was given the key of the bottomless pit. 2 And he opened the bottomless pit; and there arose a smoke out of the pit, as the smoke of a great furnace; and the sun and the air were darkened by reason of the smoke of the pit.3 And there came out of the smoke locusts upon the earth: and unto them was given power, as the scorpions of the earth have power. (Demonic spirits from the bottomless pit.) Please read Verses 1-11

Trumpet 6: /Rev 9:13-11:14 (Please read from the bible)

The sounding of the sixth trumpet reveals a vast army of 200,000 by which a third of men are killed. Even after all the war, death and destruction, verse 20-21 says that mankind still will not repent.

Trumpet 7: Rev 11:15-16:20 11:15*And the seventh angel sounded; and there were great voices in heaven saying, the kingdoms of this world are become the kingdoms of our Lord, and of His Christ; and He shall reign forever and ever. (Read the scriptures noted)*

The sounding of this last trumpet brings a pause; at which time Christ proclaims His right to rule as King of King and Lord of Lords. During this pause, other events transpire before the seven vial judgments are unleashed.

The Seven Vial Judgements

Vial 1: Rev 16:1-2 *And I heard a great voice out of the temple saying to the seven angels. Go your ways, and pour out the vials of the wrath of God upon the earth. 2 And the first went, and poured out his vial upon the earth; and there fell a noisome and grievous sore upon the men which had the mark of the beast, and upon them which worshiped his image.*

The outpouring of this vial is upon all that received the mark of the beast (666) and worship his image. The anti-christ has an image of himself put in the new temple. That is built for the Jews and demands that it is worshiped. All that received the mark, doom their souls to eternal Hell.

Vial 2: Rev 16:3 *And the second angel poured out his vial upon the sea; and it became as the blood of a dead man: and every living soul died in the sea.*

The second vial affects the oceans.

Vial 3: Rev 16:4 *And the third angel poured out his vial upon the rivers and fountains of waters; and they became blood.*

The third vial affected all the fresh water

Vial 4: Rev 16:8-9 *And the fourth angel poured out his Vial upon the sun; and power was given unto him to scorch men with fire. 9 And men were scorched with great heat, and blasphemed the name of God, which hath power over these plagues: and they repented not to give Him glory.*

This vial judgment caused the sun's rays to intensify. But the attitude of mankind did not change, as they blasphemed God instead of repenting.

Vial 5: Rev 16:10-11 *And the fifth angel poured out his vial upon the seat of the beast; and his kingdom was full of darkness; and they gnawed their tongues for pain. 11 And they blasphemed the God of heaven because of their pain and their sores. They repented not of their deeds.*

Vial 6: Rev 16:12-16 *And the sixth angel poured out his vial upon the great river Euphrates; and the water thereof was dried up, that the way of the kings of the east might be prepared. 13 And I saw three unclean spirits like frogs come out of the mouth of the dragon, and out of the mouth of the beast, and out of the mouth of the false prophet. 14 For they are the spirits of devils, working miracles, which go forth unto the kings of the earth and of the whole world, to gather them to the battle of that great day of God Almighty. 15 Behold, I come as a thief. Blessed is he that watcheth, and keepeth his garments, lest he walk naked, and they see his shame. 16*

And he gathered them together into a place called in the Hebrew tongue Armageddon.

With the Euphrates River dried up, the huge 200,000,000 army will be able to cross. This army of the anti-Christ and nations united will do battle with armies from the west and from the united group of countries supporting Israel. These armies will be gathered in a place called Armageddon to do battle. At this point, Jesus Christ returns and they all join focus to attack Him and in doing so they are destroyed.

Vial 7: Rev 16:17-21 *And the seventh angel poured out his vial into the air; and there came a great voice out of the temple of heaven, from the throne, saying, It is done. 18 And there were voices, and thunders, and lightnings; and there was a great earthquake, such as was not since men were upon the earth, so mighty an earthquake, and so great. 19 And the great city was divided into three parts, and the cities of the nations fell: and great Babylon came in remembrance before God, to give unto her the cup of the wine of the fierceness of His wrath. 20 And every island fled away, and the mountains were not found. 21 And there fell upon men a great hail out of heaven, every stone about the weight of a talent: and men blasphemed God because of the plague of the hail; for the plague thereof was exceeding great.*

Islands and mountains are not found and great hail falls from the sky. This earthquake is so huge that it affects the whole earth.

There is no knowledge of how many died in the seven year tribulation period.

1 Thes 1:10 *And to wait for His Son from heaven, whom He raised from the dead, even Jesus, WHICH DELIVERED US FROM THE WRATH TO COME.* The Church (Born again Christians) will not experience this period of time of God's wrath. The Church will have been translated to meet the Lord in the air at the start of all this.

KING JESUS RETURNS TO EARTH

At the end of the tribulation, Christ second coming will be personally, literally and visibly. This coming will be different from the rapture of the Church. The rapture can take place any moment, initiating the beginning of the tribulation—Christ will come in the air, snatch away His chosen bride in the twinkling of an eye to be with Him forever. But the Second coming is when Christ physically touches down to earth at the end of the tribulation----when Christ, who is seen by every being on earth, returns with the angels and all His saints. His return is referred to 1,845 times in the bible. His second coming is mentioned in 23 of the 27 New Testament books. Out of 260 New Testament chapters, there are 318 references to the Second Coming. Jesus Himself refers to His own return 21 times in the Gospels and believers are exhorted over fifty times to get ready for the rapture. Jesus veiled His Glory at His first coming. But when He returns, He throws off that cover and Jesus will be seen in all His majesty, it will be in a glorified body.

Rev 19:11 *I saw heaven opened, and behold, a white horse, and He who sat on it is called Faithful and True, and in righteousness He judges and wages war.*

Rev 1:7 *Behold, He is coming with the clouds, and every eye will see Him, even those who pierced Him; and all the tribes of the earth will mourn over Him. So it is to be.*

When Jesus Christ returns from Heaven to destroy the antichrist, judge the nations and establish His kingdom on earth, He will be accompanied by a great multitude. The mighty army accompanying Him will be made up of both angels and the redeemed who were raptured before the Tribulation. Before the tribulation, Christ came for His Bride (1 Thes 4:16-17 John 14:3) then, at the end of the tribulation, He will return with all His Saints. Jude 1:14 *See the Lord is coming with thousands upon thousands of His Holy Ones.* He cannot come with them until He has first come for them. The time interval between these events is seven years.

Jesus prepared the place for all the world armies to meet as Satan planned a world army attack on Israel. The three demonic spirit that proceed from the antichrist, his false prophet, and Satan himself, convinced all the world armies to converge on Israel from the signs performed by the satanic trinity.

In this location, all the worldly combatants will meet God Almighty head on in His second coming to the earth and will be destroyed. *They, (the world's armies) will make war on the Lamb, and the Lamb will conquer them, for He is Lord of Lord and King of Kings. Those with Him are called and chosen and faithful.* Jesus will put down all rebellion, both human and satanic. The two main leaders of the world, the antichrist and his false prophet, will be defeated and thrown alive into the lake of fire which burns with brimstone. Rev 19:20 *And the beast was tak-*

en, *and with him the false prophet that wrought miracles before him, with which he deceived them that had received the mark of the beast, and them that worshiped his image.* All those who followed the Antichrist and did not follow the Lord Jesus's word *"were killed with the sword which came from the mouth of Him who sat on the horse (Jesus), and all the birds were filled with their flesh"* (Rev 19:21).

This passage distinguishes between believers who were raptured at the beginning of the tribulation and unbelievers at the time of the rapture who will be left on earth to be judged during the tribulation because they chose darkness over light and salvation. Though millions will be saved during the tribulation, all on earth when the tribulation begins will be unbelievers and those who rejected the offer of salvation. 2 Thes 2:12 *That they all may be judged who did not believe the truth, but took pleasure in wickedness.*

Rev 20:1-3*And I saw an angel come down from heaven, having the key of the bottomless pit and a great chain in his hand.2 And he laid hold on the dragon, that old serpent, which is the Devil, and Satan, and bound him a thousand years,3 And cast him into the bottomless pit, and shut him up, and set a seal upon him, that he should deceive the nations no more, till the thousand years should be fulfilled: and after that he must be loosed a little season.*

Satan is bound for 1000 years, coinciding with the 1,000 year Reign of King Jesus. Under the rule of King Jesus this world will finally have peace and blessing.

Israel's Conversion

Zech 13:1 *In that day there shall be a fountain opened to the house of David and to the inhabitants of Jerusalem for sin and for uncleanness.*

Multitudes of people of Israel will be killed by the persecution of the antichrist but a remnant will be spared to receive their Messiah, whom they rejected, even at His first appearance. Because of their repenting cry out in the midst of Satan's controlling attack on God's chosen people, God heard their cry and will regather and restore a faithful Israel.

Christ Will Judge the Surviving Living

All the Gentiles and Jews alive on earth who survived the tribulation will appear before Christ that He may determine if they can enter His Kingdom. This is called the sheep goat judgement.

Matt 25:32 *All the nations will be gathered before Him; and He will separate them from one another, as the shepherd separates the sheep from the goats. Those believing, the sheep will go into the Kingdom-those unbelieving, the goats will be taken away to torment.*

CHRIST WILL RESURRECT THE DEAD

Christ will resurrect the Old Testament believers and the Tribulation saints. They will be raised, rewarded and will reign with Christ in the Kingdom in glorified bodies. The raptured church believers already have their glorified bodies and will enter the Kingdom to rule under Christ. Jesus will rule the whole earth from the new City of Jerusalem for 1000 years with all the saints ruling with Him.

SATAN IS LOOSED AFTER A THOUSAND YEARS

Rev 20:7-8 *And when the thousand years are ended, Satan shall be loosed out of his prison. 8 And shall go out to deceive the nations which are in the four quarters of the earth, Gog and Magog, to gather them together to battle, the number of whom is as the sand of the sea.*

After the 1000 years have passed in the Millennium Kingdom, Satan is let loose from the bottomless pit for a little while in order to go out and attempt to deceive the nations of the world for one last time. God allows Satan to tempt and weed out the restless bad people that were born into the millennium

Kingdom. They will all come into the city of Jerusalem to gather them together to battle; the number of whom is as the sand of the sea. But before any battle is fought, God will destroy this invading army with fire. Satan is then cast into the Lake of Fire and Brimstone where he will join the antichrist and false prophet. All three of them will remain in this place forever and ever and we will never hear from the devil again.

Even after 1000 years of universal peace after the tribulation and experiencing the Lord's goodness, people born during the milinium reign still rebelled against God. This is the final rebellion of mankind.

THE GREAT WHITE THRONE JUDGEMENT

All of unsaved humanity will now be pulled up out of Hades (hell) where they will all stand before God for their final judgment. Everyone whose name is not found written in the book of life will be thrown into the lake of fire and brimstone where they will remain forever with Satan, the Antichrist, and the False Prophet.

Rev 20:11-15 *And I saw a great white throne, and him that sat on it, from whose face the earth and the heaven fled away; and there was found no place for them. 12 And I saw the dead, small and great, stand before God; and the books were opened: and another book was opened, which is the book of life: and the dead were judged out of those things which were written in the books, according to their works. 13 And the sea gave up the dead which were in it; and death and hell delivered up the dead which were in them: and they were judged every man according to their works. 14 And death and hell were cast into the lake of fire. This is the second death. 15 And whosoever was not found written in the book of life was cast into the lake of fire.*

Every one born on earth is given the opportunity to be free from hell. Many have accused God of being cruel, but 2 Peter 2:9 says, "*It is not His will that anyone perish*". We must remember the price that was paid for God's creation to be free from hell:

John 3:16-17 *For God so loved the world, that he gave his only begotten Son, that whosoever believeth in him should not perish, but have everlasting life. 17 For God sent not his Son into the world to condemn the world; but that the world through him might be saved.*

After an unsaved person dies, they go to a place called Hades or hell. You can read all about hades or hell in Luke 16. This is the holding place for the dead, a prison. It at one time had two compartments, one was called Paradise and one called torments. After death the Old Testament Saints use to go to the paradise part because they couldn't go to heaven yet because Jesus' blood hadn't yet been shed to cover their sins. Their faith was the instrument of their being there. When Jesus was crucified, His blood finally allowed their freedom and Paradise was taken up to Heaven with Jesus after His resurrection. Those left in hell, when they are judged without the saving work of Jesus,-(the only work that matters) and our response to what Jesus did at Calvery. God gave His best to redeem mankind from sin and eternal hell. Unless Jesus work at Calvery is responded to by repentance and acceptance of His redemption plan, if you die before the rapture, you will be in hell. You will not go through the tribulation, but your final destination will be the same as those who do go through the tribulation and take the mark of the Devil. (666}

At the white thrown judgement, where they are found guilty, their final destination will be the Lake of Fire because their names were not found in the Lambs Book of life.

The New Heaven and New Earth

Our earth and heavenly atmosphere will be done away with, and in it's place we will get a new heaven and a new earth. There will no longer be any more death. The curse of Adam and Eve will have finally been broken and done away with. There will be no more sorrow, from heaven from pain, or weeping. All things will be made new. God the Father Himself will come down from heaven and dwell with man forever and ever in this new heaven and earth. We will also get the city of New Jerusalem which will come down from heaven itself. There will no longer be any temple as God and Jesus will be the temple themselves. All the nations of the earth will walk in Their light and the gates into the city will never be closed.

Rev 21:1-3 *And I saw a new heaven and a new earth: for the first heaven and the first earth were passed away; and there was no more sea. 2 And I John saw the holy city, new Jerusalem, coming down from God out of heaven, prepared as a bride adorned for her husband. 3 And I heard a great voice out of heaven saying, Behold, the tabernacle of God is with men, and he will dwell with them, and they shall be his people, and God himself shall be with them, and be their God.*

RAPTURE, READY OR NOT!

The church age will soon come to an end. This will happen on the glorious rapture day. It will be followed by God's wrath being poured out for seven years upon the earth. (Dan 9:27) Again, we know that there are many nay sayers who recognize God's merciful side, and let that misdirect their lives in which leads them to live lives that is contrary to what the word of God says is acceptable by the Lord. Those who keep God's command to endure, God will keep His word that you will be safe from the time of tribulation. As born again Christians, the bride of Christ, we are not appointed to the wrath that is coming, but to obtain salvation through our Lord and Savior Jesus Christ. 1 Thes 5:9 *For God hath not appointed us to wrath, but to obtain salvation by our Lord Jesus Christ.* God's word continually alluded to our merciful escape from the wrath that is coming upon the earth.

Luke 21:36 *Watch ye therefore, and pray always, that ye may be accounted worthy to escape all these things that shall come to pass, and to stand before the Son of man.*

The seven-year tribulation is not for rapture ready born again Christians. It is for Israel to fulfill bible prophecy and for the Gentiles (unbelievers) to be punished if they refuse to repent and accept the salvation or the Lord Jesus Christ. There are multitudes of rapture scoffers who are denying the coming prophesied rapture and the tribulation. This includes Christians and many pastors who teach that the rapture is not a reality. But as dedicated Rapture watchers we must not give up our blessed hope of the being raptured into our blessed home in heaven. It is a reality. I have included many bible scriptures with more ahead. The rapture is a reality, don't be deceived.

Rapture day is imminent! The rapture is not dependent upon heavenly signs like blood moon, comet appearance, meteorite invasion, sun or moon eclipse. These signs are only to warn or wake us up from spiritual slumber so that we will be ready for the glorious rapture. Our redemption is soon to take place. Soon and very soon, the trumpet will sound and all our trials and challenges on earth will end. We will be ushered by the Lord into our heavenly home on the imminent glorious Rapture day. We will not experience the doom and terrible ordeals of the 7 year worldwide Tribulation period. Our eternal heavenly rewards are awaiting us in heaven.

JESUS IS COMING, ARE YOU READY?

Those who are left behind after the rapture will face a world changing so rapidly they will not know what to do. Back slidden Christians will know that they missed the rapture. Those who chose not to accept the Lordship of Jesus will know what has happened. There will be multitudes who will still deny the deity of Jesus. But it won't take long before the changes being made all over the world will not be for the betterment of the world. 2 Thes 2:11-12 *And for this cause God shall send them strong delusion, that they should believe a lie: 12 That they all might be damned who believed not the truth, but had pleasure in unrighteousness.* This scripture is telling us that the power of lawlessness is currently being held in check by the Holy Spirit. After the rapture takes place, the true church is removed from the earth, and the Holy Spirit's restraint will be taken out of the way. Then there will be no born-again believers on the earth that can cry out for heaven's intervention in the things that are about to take place (The tribulation).

All the Christian workers in hospitals, nursing homes, orphanages, rescue missions, relief agencies will be gone. Every Christian law enforcement, social workers and health care will be gone. Those left behind will be subjected to those who are now under Satan's control. Many churches will be empty. Many backslidden pastors will realize that they missed the rapture and will repent, keeping their church open, but they will realize that they are all now under Satan's control of the world. This will all be the result of God's judgment on a rebellious world. (Read Rev 6-16)

If you are saved by faith in the Lord Jesus Christ, you will not be left behind in the rapture. The saved will be like the five wise virgins in Matt 25:1-13.

Matt 25:1-13 *Then shall the kingdom of the heavens be made like to ten virgins that having taken their torches, went forth to meet the bridegroom. 2 And five of them were prudent and five foolish. 3 They that were foolish took their torches and did not take oil with them; 4 but the prudent took oil in their vessels with their torches. 5 Now the bridegroom tarrying, they all grew heavy and slept. 6 But in the middle of the night there was a cry, Behold, the bridegroom; go forth to meet him. 7 Then all those virgins arose and trimmed their torches. 8 And the foolish said to the prudent, Give us of your oil, for our torches are going out. 9 But the prudent answered saying, we cannot, lest it might not suffice for us and for you. Go rather to those that sell, and buy for yourselves. 10 But as they went away to buy, the bridegroom came, and the ones that were ready went in with him to the wedding feast, and the door was shut. 11 Afterwards come also the rest of the virgins, saying, Lord, Lord, open to us; 12 but he answering said, Verily I say unto you,*

I do not know you. 13 Watch therefore, for ye know not the day nor the hour.

Don't be left behind! Made sure you are ready for the rapture. If you are still doubtful about it's reality and you are a born again Christian, I have listed some bible scriptures giving information as to it's reality. You don't want to be left behind to go through the tribulation. IT'S REAL! It is important that you put your faith in the Lord Jesus Christ as your Savior if you are not saved. If you are not sure that your relationship with the Lord is right, call on the Lord, repent for anything that you know you are involved in that can keep you on earth facing the tribulation. God is a faithful and loving God. Why would He send Jesus to earth to suffer what He went through in order to save us from the tribulation and hell if He didn't care? Unfortunately, many will not choose to be rapture ready but will choose to be wicked and unrepentant to God's call to people for salvation through Jesus Christ.

Those left behind will face a quickly changing world—and that change will not be for the better. 2 Thes 2:11 *And for this cause God shall send them strong delusion, that they should believe a lie:* The bible says that the day of salvation is today, so please do not put off this very important decision if you are not rapture ready. Pray the prayer of salvation that is listed at the end of the book. Putting this move off may be too late as Jesus could rapture His Church anytime now.

Scriptures Relating to the Rapture of the Church

John 14:2-3 *In my Father's house are many mansions: if it were not so, I would have told you. I go to prepare a place for you. 3 And if I go and prepare a place for you, I will come again, and receive you unto myself; that where I am, there ye may be also.*

Matt 24:36-39 *But of that day and hour knoweth no man, no, not the angels of heaven, but my Father only. 37 But as the days of Noe were, so shall also the coming of the Son of man be. 38 For as in the days that were before the flood they were eating and drinking, marrying and giving in marriage, until the day that Noe entered into the ark, 39 And knew not until the flood came, and took them all away; so shall also the coming of the Son of man be.*

1 Thess 4:13-15 *But I would not have you to be ignorant, brethren, concerning them which are asleep, that ye sorrow not, even as others which have no hope. 14 For if we believe that Jesus died and rose again, even so them also which sleep in Jesus will God bring with him. 15 For this we say unto you by the word of the Lord, that we which are alive and remain unto the coming of the Lord shall not prevent them which are asleep.*

1 Thess 4:16-18 *For the Lord himself shall descend from heaven with a shout, with the voice of the archangel, and with the trump of God: and the dead in Christ shall rise first: 17 Then we which are alive and remain shall be caught up together with them in the clouds, to meet the Lord in the air: and so shall we ever be with the Lord. 18 Wherefore comfort one another with these words.*

Luke 21:33-36 *Heaven and earth shall pass away: but my words shall not pass away. 34 And take heed to yourselves, lest at any time your hearts be overcharged with surfeiting, and drunkenness, and cares of this life, and so that day come upon you unawares. 35 For as a snare shall it come on all them that dwell on the face of the whole earth. 36 Watch ye therefore, and pray always, that ye may be accounted worthy to escape all these things that shall come to pass, and to stand before the Son of man.*

Matt 24:42 *Therefore, stay awake, for you do not know on what day your Lord is coming!*

Immediately after the rapture of the church, God's Spirit will remove any restraining influence on earth (2 Thess 2:7). *For the mystery of iniquity doth already work: only he who now letteth will let, until he be taken out of the way.* The best preparation for the tribulation is to make sure you're not around for it. The Word of God tells us how to live our lives in the way that is pleasing to Him. WHEN YOU PRAY THIS

PRAYER, COMMITTING YOUR LIFE TO THE LORD, WALKING IN OBEDIENCE TO HIS WORD, YOU WILL BE RAPTURE READY!

Heavenly Father, I come to You in the name of Your Son Jesus. Your Word says that whosoever shall call on the name of the Lord shall be saved. I am calling on You. For too long I have lived the way that is contrary to your word, I believe that Jesus Christ is the Son of God and that He died on the cross for my sins and rose again on the third day that I may be saved. Lord, come into my heart and make me your child. I gratefully receive Your gift of salvation. Come into my heart and be my Lord and Savior. I thank You for giving me the gift of eternal life. AMEN!

After praying the prayer of salvation, you must find a church that will help you get to know the Lord, stay committed to the Him and give you the ability to grow in your relationship with the Lord. YOU MUST STAY READY FOR THE RAPTURE!

ABOUT REV. DENOTRA JOHNSON

A former Catholic and Baptist, she spent many years running from the Lord, for fear of having a life that was unpleasant. But God had His plan for her life. After accepting the Lord in a Pentecostal church and being filled with the Holy Spirit, a life that she never dreamed of or expected was before her. After the Lord placed her in a Church, Walnut Faith Center in Pomona, California that was a powerful teaching, anointed and delivering house of God, God's anointing and calling began to manifest in and through her. As the parents of three and Grandparents they were active in the Lord's work. She was ordained as teacher in the church. After ministering at churches throughout the United States, the Lord called her to take the word and the anointing to the nations as the Evangelist.

The call was to the Philippines first, then expanded to the Orient, Singapore, China, Russian nations, Europe, Israel, Egypt, Italy and other countries where the Holy Spirit moved mightily with miracles, signs and wonders manifesting. After 12 years on the evangelistic field, the Lord called her and her husband Willard to establish a church in Apple Valley, California where they pastored for fifteen years until Willard passed away. She is now the pastor emeritus of the Church, called to stand in the officer of the prophetess, she operates in a prophetic anointing throughout the United States, crying out for the preparation of God's people for the end time. Jesus in Coming for His Church. Are you ready?

www.ingramcontent.com/pod-product-compliance
Lightning Source LLC
LaVergne TN
LVHW052001060526
838201LV00059B/3779